Anorak of Fire

The Life and Times of Gus Gascoigne, Trainspotter

A Monologue

Stephen Dinsdale

A SAMUEL FRENCH ACTING EDITION

SAMUEL FRENCH

FOUNDED 1830

SAMUELFRENCH-LONDON.CO.UK
SAMUELFRENCH.COM

ISBN 978-0-573-14201-7

www.samuelfrench-london.co.uk

www.samuelfrench.com

FOR AMATEUR PRODUCTION ENQUIRIES

UNITED KINGDOM AND WORLD EXCLUDING NORTH AMERICA
plays@SamuelFrench-London.co.uk
020 7255 4302/01

Each title is subject to availability from Samuel French,

depending upon country of performance.

ANORAK OF FIRE

THE LIFE AND TIMES OF
GUS GASCOIGNE, TRAINSPOTTER

A railway station platform

As the Curtain *rises, Gus Gascoigne is discovered. He is wearing an anorak with the hood up, school-type trousers, trainers and NHS glasses. He is carrying a notebook, biro and cheapish binoculars, and a Thermos flask and lunchbox stand nearby*

Trains can be heard passing. The sound fades after a moment

Gus I was born a spotter. Some are born, some are made. But if it's not in you, forget it. You can't bring out what isn't there. John Bagley was taken to the station every Saturday for twelve years by his dad, who was a keen spotter. A fanatical spotter. It did no good. It didn't take. It wasn't in him. He went to fishing and that is still like a religion to him. But me. I can still remember when I saw my first loco. I must have still been in the pram. It wasn't so much the sight of it — I probably couldn't have seen it as I was in the pram — but it was the feel of it. The feel of its presence. It's hard to explain but from that moment I was hooked. I still get that feeling to this day. To this day. The funny thing is, I can't remember what that loco was — the one that made me a pram convert — and I think I ought to be able to. It was a traction unit of some kind but the exact specification escapes me. But you ask me any other. Any other since that moment and I could tell you. I've got one of the best spotting memories in the country. Known for it. If there was a Mastermind for spotters I'd walk it. There's this bloke in Manchester. Eric Spate. Fancies himself as a bit of a memory. He's got his own little gang — the Manchester Maf. I let it be known that I'd meet him in Crewe. Just a friendly, you know, see who's really best. I wasn't worried. Come the day I blew him off the platform. You're talking to the best here. Proven.

It was difficult for me at first. I was the only spotter in our street. That's quite unusual. There are more of us than you think, you know. And my dad wasn't a spotter. He was a leek man. Grew leeks. Still does. No encouragement there. But from the moment I could walk I'd be off to the station. I'd be ever running down to the station to watch the trains go by. I knew the exact times by the time I was three. It was only a small station so there weren't any other spotters there and our mum thought it was weird. I used to bunk off kindergarten to go down there and once I was almost run over by a milk float. When that happened our mum took me to see a psychologist or a truant officer or something like that. Well, she was going to, only Uncle Henry, who had this hardware shop, said, "Don't be silly, it's just a phase," so she didn't. I don't remember that. Uncle Henry told me before he died. He was a ferret man, was Uncle Henry, so he knew a bit about what was going on. He did take an interest. He gave me this picture of the Mallard once, the one with it going through a tunnel. You know it? It's quite well known. Quite famous.

Anyway I was a lone spotter down at this little station till I was about six. I didn't have a notebook or anything. Just watched the trains. The station staff all knew me and made me cups of tea and gave me KitKats. And because they knew me our mum didn't worry so much and let me spend more time down there and didn't keep fetching me back. I didn't run from school so much and I drew a lot of train pictures there. My seventh birthday was the turning point. The watershed. My parents didn't have much money and I hadn't been out of town much except for in buses which don't count.

Did you know there are bus spotters? I couldn't believe it either — makes you laugh, doesn't it? Bus spotters! It's true! Anyway we went to see our Aunt Jenny who lives in Crewe and we went by train. It was my first proper train journey. The only other one I'd been on was the local line to the next town for Saturday shopping which was only a rail bus, you know, nothing interesting at all. So on my seventh birthday we took the train to Crewe. We'd never have left the station if our dad hadn't carried me. Aunt Jenny couldn't understand it. She thought I didn't like her. I cried all day and refused any seed cake. I wanted to be back at that station. You see, Crewe station for the spotter is like Monte Carlo for James Bond. For a while, on that day, at the age of seven, I was in Heaven. And I did not want to leave.

What's the line in that David Bowie song? "No, no, you're not alone!" I know what he meant now. I hadn't heard the song then, not properly, because I was seven and I wasn't into rock. I am now — I like Thrash Metal — but what I mean is, I know that feeling. Suddenly you find you're not alone. I will never forget coming into Crewe station and seeing that platform. Thick with spotters. Thick with them. Our mum saw them first and tried to cover my face with her coat but it was no good. You could hardly miss them. There were more spotters than passengers. I couldn't believe it. I didn't realize, at first, that they were spotters. Then this Deltic (that's a loco) came in and they all surged to the other side of the platform with notebooks and cameras. If the platform had been a ship it would have capsized. Without realizing what I was doing I went over with them. It was a wonderful feeling.

And this bloke, he must have been about forty if he was a day, he was next to me and he looked at me and the look said, "You and I understand each other. I may be forty and you may be seven but here we are equals," and that was it. He didn't say anything but that was it. Then our mum came and gave me a clout round the head for running away even if was my birthday and then she cried because she regretted it and I felt sorry for her and tried to explain that I couldn't help it and then our dad bought us all a cup of tea. But from that moment on I was lost to them. And they could not get me off that platform.

Of course, I wanted to be an engine driver. Most spotters do. But our dad wasn't having that. I got GCSEs. If I'd realized the implications I wouldn't have bothered. I'd have spotted instead of swotted. Haha. Our dad made that up. But I got them and it was white collar work for me. "I didn't bring you up with the sweat of my brow and go without so that you can swan off and work with a lot of Bongos and Pakis," he said. I never saw him sweat — he worked in the Civil Service doing something or other and I've no idea what he went without because if he wasn't at work he'd be with his leeks. He didn't have time to go without anything. I don't think we went without. Anyway I went into computing. A lot of spotters work in computing. I don't know why that is but it's a statistical fact. I'd got maths and CDT, physics, chemistry. Computers were about the only growth industry round here so I went to tech college. Did computing. I've left out all my schooldays, haven't I? There's not much to tell. I'd go to school in the morning, come home and spot, do my homework and spot and go to bed. I already told you my best subjects. I didn't like sport much. Football was boring. I quite liked cricket because if you got to bat first, you could sneak off behind the sightscreen and bunk off to the railway cutting which was quite nearby. I was out first ball a lot. I saw my first electric conversion on one of those days. The excitement is hard to describe. I'll always remember it because when I saw it I came back to the field to tell my friend Kevin who was another spotter and fielding for the other side at mid on. I yelled about it to him and he was hit straight in the testicles by a really hard ball that John Rainer batted. It was quite funny really. He's an estate agent now.

Funny word that, testicles. Father Bob, our parish priest, calls them testimonials. Father Bob is quite a remarkable man. He's a spotter. That is unusual. A spotter priest. He's more an armchair spotter though, because his parish duties are so arduous he has little time for spotting. He has Tuesday evenings off and he's down the station then quite often. But usually he just talks to us about it. Asks us what we've seen. I don't go to church but he's often in the graveyard doing something or other as I go by and he'll shout, "Did you see seven-five-six-two-five-four?" and I'll say "Yes!" or "No!" and he'll be pleased. Or not. I know for a fact that he composes his sermons listening to tapes of Castle Class steamers in Kent because I heard him on more than one occasion. Just this one time I remember he tried to bring spotting into the sermon, describing Christ as the spotter of men and life being like a track with a third rail, but I never really understood it. I went to church especially to hear it because he told us spotters he was going to give it a try but I'm not sure that it was a success. He certainly didn't repeat it. Whereas his goldfish one, in which he likens life to a goldfish bowl and we're all either tench or mullet is very popular and he does it about once a month. With variations. He has this moped too and he drives it quite fast from the hospital to the Oxfam Shop and wherever else priests go. But he is a keen spotter — forever asking me how it's going. He doesn't get down to the track often actually. In fact, I've only seen him the once. But he is keen. He speaks the language. We can — relate. And when people, our mum especially, criticize and point the finger at us for indulging in our harmless hobby we can say "Father Bob does it" — and that shuts them up.

Actually our mum is not all that religious but she would never admit that. She never goes to church except to Midnight Mass on Christmas Eve and she always gets the time wrong. Does it start at midnight or end at midnight? She can never remember. One year there was trouble because she wanted me to go with her and I wanted to go to the Christmas Eve all-night spot — which is always full of surprises and the odd shock because the timetables change due to the holiday rostering. You never know what might come along and that, of course, is the attraction. Plus carol singing round the brazier. Well, there should be a brazier but the police usually get us to put it out. The station staff don't mind. Not on our station. All right, we've never actually had a brazier but this year we're definitely going to try. We can disguise it as a litter bin. I bet the filth do try and make us put it out though. The filth. Ha. Anyway, the upshot was, of course, that I went to the service to keep on the good side of our mum and because, after all, it was Christmas. Perhaps you could say I was paying her back for all the packed lunches over the year. What I thought would be worse was that we knew, some of us, pretty well for sure, that a certain loco from Southern Region, number two-five-three-four-five-seven City of Maidstone, would be hauling a train through ours at about eleven-forty-five p.m. that very Christmas Eve night because they had got their holiday schedules buggered up. Our lot, not Southern Region. Southern Region don't bugger up much, I've heard. Very efficient, Southern. Must be quite a boring place to spot. Anyway, to spot that loco at ours would be big news indeed. And where would I be? In pigging church. I'd hoped to keep it quiet that I was in church but it got out. Our mum again. She's got this thing going with Mrs Timmins whose husband is big in the Co-Op — and he's in the Rotary — about whatdoyoucallit? Beggar my neighbour. She's not our neighbour, Mrs Bott is, the one with the pink hat and the piles — but it's that kind of thing. She has to be one better. "Your Jeremy coming to the service, Phoebe?" she says to her in the library, where she goes for her Georgette Heyer. "My Gus will be there. He always comes." Of course she's only got her snotty kid Philamon with her and his brother Tobit is a spotter. Creepy bastard. So he comes down and spreads it round — "Gus will be in church on the twenty-fourth, everyone. Better take a photo for him." That was a bit embarrassing, because I'd told them all I was going down to Crewe.

But night-spotting can be totally, totally weird. It's dark.

The Lights dim

You are alone. Just you, your notebook, your lunchbox and your anorak. It's a bit like in *Jaws* when they're floating along in that boat dropping bait and waiting for the shark to appear and nothing's happening. And then suddenly it does. Appear. The best place to go night-spotting is outside a tunnel. You're not supposed to of course. It's not permitted. It's out of bounds to all unauthorized personnel. But my biggest kicks have come from waiting on the embankment outside a tunnel in the pitch black. It's best to have one trusted companion with you but you get a special thrill when you're alone. It's dead, dead quiet. I always think of all those Victorian navvies that hewed the tunnel out of the living rock. How can rock be living? And if that's living rock, what's dead rock? Mick Jagger, I suppose.

Haha. Sh! I think of those Westerns where the Indian puts his ear to the rail and can hear the train coming miles and miles away. I'd like to try that but it's a bit dangerous and in a way it would spoil it because it's the element of surprise that you go for. Then you try to lean towards the tunnel to see if you can hear anything. If it's a windy night there will be a low sort of howling sound then, mixed in with it, was that a rumble of a different kind? You feel for your notebook. It's there, reassuring, in the lining of your anorak. Is it the distant beat of a diesel engine or is it just your heart pounding? There is something! No — the brain becomes confused as the wind buffets your head as it whistles through the tunnel. You become lost in a confusion of sound, you don't know what it is, you are sucked into a whirlpool of echoes. Suddenly you hear it. A rhythmic beat of diesel, without a doubt! You grab your book, you brace yourself! Only the roar of the wind!

He pauses

That can happen so often on a night spot. Sometimes you can wait for hours and nothing happens except you get slowly colder.

There is an enormous roar and a strobe light effect for about six seconds

Intercity one-two-five number five-six-eight-six-seven-five Leicester City! Did you get it? You are slow. I don't think you'd make very good spotters. You need training up. I could feel it coming. I knew it was coming. It's something you can't learn. It's innate. Intercity one-two-fives are the best though. They sort out the sheep from the lambs. On a platform you can't stand too near them or you get sucked under. And they are very fast, as you just saw. They can take you by surprise. Unless you can feel them coming. Like me.

The Lights get brighter so that Gus can be seen more clearly

Night-spotters are the *crème de la crème* of trainspotters. You have to be truly dedicated, let's face it. But the dedication can pay off. I think every night-spotter has a strange tale to tell. For instance I heard a couple of signalmen talking a few months back about a certain diesel unit, the specification of which I won't bore you with because it will mean nothing to you, but a special unit which you just will not see in our region at all, normally. Not at all! What a coup! They were obviously keeping this to themselves because nobody else knew about it and I wasn't telling. I felt like those American reporters in Watergate. This unit would be hauling a freight train on a track not usually used for freight. It was a commuter track, a suburban line going through all the housing estates and that. And this special unit, diesel, mind you, not electric, would only come through at three a.m., so, like I said, I kept shtum.

I wanted to be the only one in ours to know about this unit. Did not breathe a word. I remember thinking how secretive the two signal-men looked. I've seen that look before — on Wally Bacon's dad's face when we caught him coming out of *Night of the Swedish Virgins* after an all-night spot. I mean he hadn't been on an all-night spot. We had. The look on his face was the look on these signal-men's. And they talked about it getting out to the press. I suppose they meant *Spotters' Weekly* and, yes, it would have been news. These units were rare. Very rare. As I said. Anyway, come the night I slipped out of the house without waking our mum. Our mum is funny about night-spotting. She used to think ... it's embarrassing! Well, I suppose you can imagine what she thought if you look at it from her point of view. She used to think I was going with a girl. Ever since I helped Doreen Lipfield with her maths our mum's been funny like that. I don't even like Doreen Lipfield. She's fat. And she's got spots. I know I have but that's just acne. Doreen's got proper spots. I don't think she washes and she eats the wrong food. Anyway our mum thought I was seeing girls on night-spots and one night — oh, the embarrassment — she followed me and hid behind the GPO van near the station. Half an hour was enough. The cold drew her out. She pretended she had just been passing by but nobody believed her at half-past twelve at night and I was a laughing stock. But the thing with our mum is that she will have the last word and as she walked away she sort of half shouted "Doreen! I know you're there!" to a group of grown spotters killing themselves laughing at me! I could have strangled her!

Anyway the upshot is that I don't tell her about night-spots now. I just slip out. And that's what I did on the night of this special freight train. I went down to the cutting at Harbottle Street and shinned up Mrs Packhurst's maple tree which is the best spotting position in Yorkshire if you ask my opinion. I settled to wait and I had my camera ready to photograph this unit. Exposure in the press did suggest itself to me, especially after what those signalmen had said. It was two forty-five when I went up that tree which gave me fifteen minutes to wait if it was on time. I shall never forget that night. It is etched on my memory like losing my virginity probably would have been if I had lost it. As it came up the line I thought it sounded funny. I can't put my finger on it. Just sort of different. And then it came into view, slowly, very slowly. I could not believe my eyes. My camera finger clicked and clicked blindly. It was a train carrying nuclear waste and coming through our little station! I knew I'd get the front page on *Spotters' Weekly* for sure! Because there were *two* of those units pulling it! Two! I got about twenty pictures of them. They were brilliant. I don't think two of those units had ever been seen together before. And next month, there they were on the cover of *Spotters' Weekly*. My photo. Taken by me. Got a fiver for that. Even the Young Liberals were interested. They came round and asked to see my photos but they didn't seem to find them very interesting when they saw them. They wanted pictures of the nuclear stuff and I didn't have those. You have to keep politics out of spotting or it ruins it. Spotting is a great leveller. The way sport used to be. There's a laugh. But spotting really is a brotherhood of man.

It is true, though, what Claire Rayner says. It is hard to spot and have what they call a relationship. Spotting is a closed world. Not very attractive to women. I don't know why. But who understands 'em, eh, chaps? Not us, eh, eh? That's for sure. Our dad is always saying that. There are some women spotters but it's hard for them to spot and bring up a family so mothers don't seem to encourage it in their daughters — certainly not round our way. Few spotters have what you would call an active relationship with the opposite sex. Some of the older ones are married but I think it still applies. The wives find other outlets — macramé for example. Whatever that is. I hear

it mentioned. A lot of the older ones are still single. John Thwaite
and his whippet still live at home and his mum is ninety if she's a
day. He's about forty-five. He fishes too. There's some conflict
there, with the spotting. And he's in the Rotary. A very full life. No
time for a wife. It's happening everywhere you know, if you look
at the statistics. Marriages failing, birth-rate falling. Spotting in-
creasing — oh, it is you know — there's a connection. And you can't
get AIDS standing by a railway track.

Anyway I can give you a real life example of true love thwarted,
blighted and star-crossed through spotting. Step forward Gus Clive
Gascoigne! Ta-da! This happened quite recently. It's a bit hard to
talk about but we must all make sacrifices for what we hold dear and
I want to try and bare myself — for the sake of greater understanding
of spotting and its joys and sacrifices. I was after this particular
traction unit. A diesel. I kept missing it for one reason or another.
Sod's law. What was worse was that it had a distinctive kind of low
whistle. (*He makes a humming noise*) I heard it twice but for one
reason or another was unable to actually spot it. Once, for example,
it passed behind a high wall and I couldn't see it. Get the picture? It
began to haunt me. Everyone I knew had spotted it, some about eight
times, and they began to take the piss. I kept hearing that whistle —
(*he makes the humming noise again*) — even in my dreams. Please
remember that.

Not long ago my flask broke. I dropped it in surprise when the five-
nineteen from Manchester arrived on time one Thursday. So I had
to get a new one so our mum wouldn't know I'd dropped it. Made
quite a dent in my allowance — our mum takes my wages and gives
me an allowance. The rest goes on my keep and in the savings book.
Quite sensible really. So I went to Boots and asked for one identical
and then I said to the girl as a joke, not really meaning anything
serious, "Can I pay for it in instalments?" "Yes," she says and gives
me this very funny look. Then her mate, who is standing next to her
at the till, you know the way they do — can't be cost effective —
pisses herself laughing. So I said, "Right. Here's fifty p. You can
have the rest next week." Silly cow. So then her mate says "Only if

you take her" — not the mate, the other one — "to the pictures on Saturday." So I was a bit red now because they were obviously taking the piss but I said, "What's on then?" They said they didn't know. Well, that's stupid because what's the point of going if you don't know what's on? So she said — that's the mate said — "How about going to the Sunset Cinema Club?" and we all know what they put on there! So I said, "No, not my cup of tea," so the mate says, "Are you a poof?" So I said "No!" So she says, "Well take her" — that's the first one — "out on Saturday to prove it," so I sort of agreed. I was still two pounds fifty up because I'd got the flask on tick and I thought I could get out of Saturday especially when I heard the second one say the first one owed her a quid. It had all been a bet anyway. I felt a right prat. I put Saturday out of my mind. Unfortunately I bumped into the friend on the Friday who said that her friend whose name was Jacky would be waiting for me on Saturday under the stone cross and I'd better be there or there'd be trouble!

And I began to think, well, why not? She wasn't bad looking and the film was *Conan the Barbarian Strikes Back* which I wanted to see anyway so I thought, "Get it over", and I went. We got on surprisingly well. I didn't know what to do really because to tell you the truth what with schoolwork, spotting and then paid work and spotting I hadn't really had time for girls — like I told you, there just isn't any — so I didn't know if she wanted me to snog her or anything so I didn't. I sort of put my arm half round her — up on the seat like that and left it there as a gesture. You know, that I wasn't a poof. And I bought her an ice-cream which she liked. Then afterwards she said how about walking me to the bus stop, so I do and as soon as we get there her mate Natalie turns up out of nowhere. So I thought "Time to go," but they wouldn't have that and I had to sit between them and answer millions of questions, mostly from Natalie who was very nosy and of course the spotting soon came out. After they had pissed themselves laughing for about five minutes I said to Jacky, "Look, I came to the pictures with you" — *Conan the Barbarian* was crap by the way. The books and comics are far better — "you've got to come spotting with me. It's only fair," I said. She wanted to bring Natalie. I put my foot down. I said, "No way. She didn't come to the pictures, did she?" They couldn't answer that of course. And I also said if she didn't come she couldn't have her two pound fifty I still owed her. That was a bit below the belt but at least I was getting my own back, wasn't I? So in the end she had to come. I thought the next Sunday would be a good day because of course she worked on the Saturday but she was having none of that. Sunday was ballroom dancing for her. That was a close one I thought — it could have been dancing instead of Conan — so it's a Saturday night night-spot in the end, isn't it? She agreed quite readily which I thought strange as I would have thought a novice would have preferred to start in daylight. She said was I fully equipped and remember she worked in Boots. I said the new flask was fine and she gave me another of those funny looks.

Come the night I was ready. I was still hoping to spot that loco I told you about before and I had been informed that it was somewhere in the neighbourhood so the evening could be described as full of promise. I didn't think she'd turn up. Come six o'clock she's there. You should have seen what she was wearing! What a wally. She had boots with high heels that came up to here — (*he indicates*) — and a miniskirt on! She had a top that hardly covered her whatsits and a sort of short leather jacket. I said to her "You're going to freeze." "Oh no I'm not," she says, and comes out with that look again. So we settle down to spot. She hasn't brought a notebook, has she? I give her a couple of sheets of mine but she keeps losing them in the wind. I say "Well, write them on your hand; lots of spotters do that if a loco takes them by surprise and then transfer them to their books later." "Nice idea," she says but she can't ruin her hands. She'd better write them on her leg. "Don't be stupid," I say, "your tights will get in the way." "I'm not wearing them," she says. "It's stockings," and do I want her to show me? And half the station watching. I say, "No," I believe her and that I'll take the numbers down for her. Then she gets bored and says can she take the numbers down for me. I say "OK," and the next train that comes in she misses completely and the one after that she only goes and puts it round the wrong way. I think she did it on purpose. She's obviously getting bored and spotting is definitely not for her. We waste half an hour drinking coffee in the buffet and I decide to tell her to go and forget the whole thing when she says she knows this perfect place for spotting which is a lot warmer. She says that Tim Bixton told her about it. Now she's got me believing that because Tim Bixton was a spotter of some repute, though why he should tell her about it is beyond me. He was rather a strange spotter, was Tim — kept himself to himself and always carried a mysterious pale green lunchbox. He often produced some very fine photographs and we all knew he had discovered a good hide somewhere that none of us knew about. And this Jacky knew where it was. I asked her how she knew but she laughed again. She said to follow her and I'd find out.

So I followed her out of the station and down the High Street away from the railway which I thought a bit strange and down to the off-licence where she got a couple of bottles of cider, to keep us warm, she said. I said, "I've got some tea in the flask," but no, it had to be cider. Then we were off again down a side alley and back towards the main line. Next to it was this little wood which is fenced off. You can't get into it. Only you can. Inside this little wood was a sheltered clearing with a perfect view of the track. I could tell Tim had been there because there were some empty film canisters lying about — the type he uses. The grass was all squashed down and there were cigarette ends lying about. Tim smokes. He's that kind of idiot. Anyway, it was pretty good really, I have to say, and I lay down on my stomach and I was practically looking straight out on to the track. Perfect for spotting. I said "Thanks Jacky, I didn't know you cared." And she said, "But I do," and she jumped on me and stuck her tongue down my throat again as they say in the books. I thought, "Oh no, here I am in this perfect spotting place and I've got this rampant female to cope with." I wished she'd go away but I could hardly say that when she'd shown me the place so we snogged for a bit and I hoped that would keep her quiet. No. One and a half bottles of cider disappeared down her neck while I observed two goods trains and a one-two-five, all of which I'd seen before. No sign of the one I was after, needless to say. I kept my ears peeled for its special whistle — (*he makes the humming noise*) — but nothing. She goes quiet for a bit — she'd been asking all sorts of stupid questions and putting me off my stride — and I was just getting ready to note what was hauling the ten-fifteen from Workington when she says "Gus." I look round

and there she is, stark, bollock, naked. She just stands there and
looks at me. Half of me thought "Oh, no, if this ever gets out," and
the other half thought, "Cor, well, why not, you know, I mean —
yeah." I couldn't really believe it. So then, of course, she starts
undressing me and saying the most filthy things; I didn't really
know what to do but before long we're both in our birthday suits. I'm
just so glad it was dark. But I was too shocked to be embarrassed.
I said to her "Have you done this before?" She just laughs and she
pulls me down to, you know, do the business. Then she starts
moaning and wriggling and panting and gasping and then just as I'm
about to, you know, stick it in, like I've read about, she lets go this
really low moan — (*he makes the humming noise*) — turned on, you
know. Well, this moan is exactly like the whistle of that loco I was
telling you about. I thought it was coming and jumped up to spot it
and that was it, really. Our relationship couldn't take the strain.
When I realized it wasn't the loco I was a bit pissed off and wasn't
in the mood any more. You know, rise to the occasion, like. And I
could tell she was a bit pissed off. Because she did. Piss off, I mean.
So I just settled down to a nice night-spot. It was a great place to do
it. Incidentally, between spots I looked at some of Tim's used film
cartridges. They were full of used thingies. Quite disgusting really.

Anyway that is a good example of how spotting can ruin a
relationship.

You may have noticed that I am wearing an anorak. A lot of spotters
do. This has been commented on in the popular press on more than
one occasion. I thought this would be a good opportunity to explain
to you one or two reasons why we wear the things we do.

To begin with: sneakers, trainers, call them what you will. These
enable the spotter to flash from one side or even end of the
platform to another when two sought-after locos should appear
simultaneously.

Trousers. Tricky one, this. Some of the new strain of spotter, the
unweaned and trendy perhaps, will wear jeans. I say no, no, no.

Spotting is a dignified, at best almost scholarly occupation. I think jeans create totally the wrong impression. A spotter should look smart ... ish. Presentable, ready to mix with all strata of society.

The lunchbox. Always discreet and well packed. The spotter's mother or wife is, of course, responsible for this. Usually the mother.

The notebook. Plain cover. Never flowers or Garfield.

Woolly hat. You may laugh but you try standing on a night-spot in the middle of the Pennines without one. Not in football colours *please*. You can get mixed up with supporters on a platform and several nasty accidents have occurred as a consequence.

Finally — the anorak. I am very proud of this one. I can confidently say that you will not find a better one anywhere. There is a story attached to it which I will tell you in a minute. This one is very old — nineteen-fifties, from the age of steam spotting. Seen a lot of action. Good deep pockets. Get loads of cameras and sandwiches in there. Good strong hood. Zips and things everywhere. And the badges of course. Down each side. Some of these are very old and valuable. People say, "Gus — leave them at home. They are too valuable to risk." I say, "No. I have a responsibility to get them seen. I do not own them. I just look after them and will pass them on to He Who Follows Me." You see, this anorak belonged to Jim O'Rourke. Yes, I thought there would be a ripple of amazement. *The* Jim O'Rourke. The one who appeared on *What's My Line?* in nineteen sixty-six. I'd thought you'd remember him. He was a chicken-catcher and nobody could guess what he did except Dame Anne thingy who came close, apparently. So he's very famous in our town for having been on telly and beating the panel in *What's My Line?* It was before my time of course, but they still talk about it. Anyway, Jim O'Rourke was a famous spotter and owned this anorak, with its badges which he had collected over the years and when I first started spotting he took me under his wing and taught me all he knew — well, as much as a genius like that can teach you all he knows. He took me through night-spotting survival, the flying spot, which you do from a bridge, the reverse drop spot with two notebooks which you can only really do at Crewe because you need three platforms, mirror spotting, and the famous elliptical whistle spot which involves some study of Zen and is far too complex to describe here. Suffice it to say that O'Rourke, if he needed a number badly enough, could even spot a loco that to a less developed eye *was not even there*. Deep waters, deep waters. And I was his faithful pupil and hung on his every word. And he respected this and said "Gus. I cannot spot forever. One day I will have to stop. And when I do I want this anorak to be yours." And he would run his hands over the lapels and stroke the badges. And I was honoured. And proud. He died sooner than we all expected. He was not a young man and chicken-catching is a young man's game. One day a particularly spirited chicken had his name on it and ran him into the ground. He caught it, but it was to be his last. But his memory, his legacy, lives on in the anorak he left me. And here it is: my Godly Sheath, my Golden Fleece, my Anorak of Fire! I was in two minds as to whether or not to wash it. I mean, if I did, would I be wiping off all traces of Jim's aura? On the other hand it was covered in his dog's doings and what not. In the end I left it. Doesn't smell too bad. And ever since I've had it my life's taken on new purpose. New meaning. He's with me, yeah, I know he's with me. Sometimes on a cold Pennine night, under the stars, when the rails are humming with I know not what, I like to think I can feel him in the lining. Yeah — bit of poetry there, but justified, I think.

All this talk of anoraks — it's got my spotting blood up. It's a great feeling; I wish I could share it with you, but like I say, it's either there or it's not. I was just thinking, I could still catch that new one-two-five I've been promising myself. Right. That's it. The call of the track. No more talk — action. It's been very nice, but I can only stay away for so long, then I start to get itchy. Stay if you want, but don't say I didn't warn you — you might get hooked.

CURTAIN

FURNITURE AND PROPERTY LIST

On stage: Thermos flask
                 Lunchbox

Personal: **Gus:** notebook, biro, cheapish binoculars

LIGHTING PLOT

Practical fittings required: nil

A railway platform. The same scene throughout

To open: Full general lighting

Cue 1	**Gus**: "It's dark." *Dim lights*	(Page 6)
Cue 2	**Gus**: " ... you get slowly colder." *Strobe light effect*	(Page 7)
Cue 3	**Gus**: "Like me." *Bring lights up brighter*	(Page 7)

EFFECTS PLOT

Cue 1   As Curtain rises   (Page 1)
Train noises in background; fade when ready

Cue 2   **Gus**: " ... you get slowly colder."   (Page 7)
Enormous roar

www.ingramcontent.com/pod-product-compliance
Ingram Content Group UK Ltd.
Pitfield, Milton Keynes, MK11 3LW, UK
UKHW021818150726
7214IPUK00017B/193